DATE DUE		

DISCARD

SMOKIN'
OPEN-WHEEL
RACE CARS

FAST WHEELS!

ERIN EGAN

Speeding Star

an imprint of
Enslow Publishers, Inc.

Copyright © 2014 Enslow Publishers, Inc.

Originally published as *Hottest Race Cars* © 2008 Enslow Publishers, Inc.

Speeding Star, an imprint of Enslow Publishers, Inc.

Library of Congress Cataloging-in-Publication Data

Egan, Erin.

 Smokin' open-wheel race cars / Erin Egan.
  pages cm. — (Fast wheels!)
 Previously titled: Hottest race cars
 Includes bibliographical references and index.
 Summary: "Read about open-wheel race cars, the drivers, and the races they compete in, such as
Formula One and the IZOD IndyCar Series"—Provided by publisher.
 ISBN 978-1-62285-100-3
 1. Automobile racing--Juvenile literature. 2. Automobiles, Racing—Juvenile literature. I. Title.
 GV1029.13.E43 2013
 796.72—dc23
                                        2012048119

Future Editions:
Paperback ISBN: 978-1-62285-101-0
EPUB ISBN: 978-1-62285-103-4
Single-User PDF ISBN: 978-1-62285-104-1
Multi-User PDF ISBN: 978-1-62285-163-8

Printed in the United States of America

072013 Lake Book Manufacturing, Inc., Melrose Park, IL

10 9 8 7 6 5 4 3 2 1

To Our Readers: We have done our best to make sure all Internet addresses in this book were active and
appropriate when we went to press. However, the author and the Publisher have no control over, and assume
no liability for, the material available on those Internet sites or on other Web sites they may link to. Any com-
ments or suggestions can be sent by e-mail to comments@speedingstar.com or to the following address:

Speeding Star
Box 398, 40 Industrial Road
Berkeley Heights, NJ 07922
USA
www.speedingstar.com

Photo Credits: anson/Shutterstock.com, p. 23; AP Images/Ben Margot, p. 40 (bottom left); AP Images/David
Davies/PA Wire, p.25; AP Images/Ferrari.com, p. 21; AP Images/Larry Papke, p. 38; AP Images/Luca Bruno, p. 26;
AP Images/Mark Duncan, p. 44; AP Images/Michael Conroy, p. 14; AP Images/PA Wire, p. 27; AP Images/Walter
G Arce/Cal Sports Media, p. 29; BBurcham/Shutterstock.com, p. 17; CHEN WS/Shutterstock.com, p. 34; © Corel
Corporation, p. 31; Darren Brode/Shutterstock.com, p. 12; David Acosta Allely/Shutterstock.com, p. 22 (left);
Dennis Steen/Shutterstock.com, p.12 (left); Efecreata Photography/Shutterstock.com, pp. 7, 10, 39; Francesco
Dazzi/Shutterstock.com, p. 36 (bottom); Hodag Media/Shutterstock.com, p. 22 (right); Lori Carpenter/Shutter-
stock.com, pp. 19, 40 (top right); Natursports/Shutterstock.com, p. 4; Oskar SCHULER/Shutterstock.com, p. 33;
Photo Works/Shutterstock.com, p. 12 (right); Richard Lyons/Shutterstock.com, p. 12; Sandra R. Barba/Shutter-
stock.com, p. 8; Sergei Bachlakov/Shutterstock.com, p. 13; Tatiana Popova/Shutterstock.com, p. 36 (top)

Cover Photo: BBurcham/Shutterstock.com

CONTENTS

Kamui Kobayashi is shown at the Circuit de Catalunya in Barcelona, Spain. He is going so fast that his head feels five times heavier than normal!

OPEN-WHEEL RACING

It is May 27, 2012, at the Indianapolis Motor Speedway, the largest sports arena in America. More than 300,000 people roar with excitement as sleek, colorful cars speed around the track during the Indy 500. The powerful race cars hug the ground as they whip around the steeply banked corners. Their engines fill the air with an ear-rattling buzz that sounds like a huge swarm of killer bees. The cars are a blur as they travel at more than 200 miles per hour (mph). Even at those high speeds, the cars are inches apart as they head around the final turn, with the finish line dead ahead. At the last moment, one car jumps ahead and everyone is on their feet as the checkered flag is waved—Dario Franchitti, has won the world's most famous car race!

It was not any ordinary victory. Franchitti was battling his teammate, Scott Dixon, and another driver, Takuma Sato during the last five laps of the race. Takuma's tires rubbed Dario's and it sent him into the wall. Franchitti and Dixon continually kept stealing the lead from one another until the final lap when Franchitti did not look back. It wasn't just the race that was extraordinary, it was the whole day. This was the first Indy 500 since the death of Dan Wheldon, the prior year's winner of the prestigious race. The drivers who finished first, second, and third, Dario Franchitti, Scott Dixon, and Tony Kanaan, were Dan's best friends.

OPEN WHEELS

The lean, mean race cars in the Indy 500 are known as open-wheel racers. They are called "open wheel" because there are no fenders covering the tires as on regular passenger cars. They are lightweight and aerodynamic (designed to cut cleanly through the air), and have extremely powerful engines. They average speeds from 187 to 220 mph. Open-wheel vehicles are raced in Formula One, Indy Racing League, and Champ Series races.

The cars hold a single driver in an open cockpit. Formula One, Indy, and Champ cars also have their engines in the back. By comparison, the cars of NASCAR have their engines in the front, and their drivers are enclosed inside the car.

FORMULA ONE

The "formula" in Formula One is the set of rules all of its drivers and cars must follow. Formula One is extremely popular around the world, especially in Europe. Its drivers come from all over the globe—Europe, North and South America, and Asia. They are as famous as rock stars, and

Wheels are not the only things exposed on an open-wheel race car. The driver, in this case Fernando Alonso, sits in an open cockpit.

THE BEST OF THE BEST

Every sport has its share of superstars, but there always seems to be one or two of them who shine brighter than all the rest. Basketball has Michael Jordan. Baseball has Babe Ruth. Hockey has Wayne Gretzky. And Formula One racing has Michael Schumacher as its super-superstar.

Schumacher won seven Formula One championships in his career—the most of any driver in history. Five of those were won while racing for the Ferrari team.

When Schumacher joined the team in 1996, Ferrari had not won a championship since 1979. In just a few years, the German driver turned the team around. With Schumacher at the wheel, Ferrari won five straight titles, from 2000 to 2004.

Until his second retirement following the 2012 season, Schumacher was one of the world's most famous athletes. His outstanding success on the track, including records for most race wins and most season championships, helped him earn more than $80 million a year in his prime.

hundreds of thousands of die-hard fans pack the tracks on race weekends worldwide. The average weekend attendance for a Formula One race is roughly 300,000 people. That is nearly triple the number of people who attended Super Bowl XLI in 2011, when 103,219 people attended the game. Television ratings top more than 100 million viewers worldwide.

Anywhere from seventeen to twenty races make up the Formula One season. In each race, twenty-four drivers compete on specially designed racecourses or blocked-off city streets. Races are held all around the world. Drivers earn points in each race depending on how they finish, and the driver with the most points at the end of the season is the champion.

Drivers race for teams, which are often owned by car companies such as Ferrari, Renault, Mercedes, Lotus, and BMW. These sponsors pay for the car as well as salaries for the drivers and crew members. The sponsors' names are painted on the car. The more money they pay, the bigger their name appears on the car. Sponsors want fans to know their names so they will buy their products. After all, running a Formula One team is not cheap—it can cost from $120 million to over $400 million a year.

FROM GRAND PRIX TO FORMULA ONE

Formula One was once officially known as Grand Prix racing. *Grand Prix* is a French term for "large prize." The first Grand Prix race was held in Le Mans, France, in 1906, but it was only open to French drivers. The first Grand Prix World Championship was held in 1925, but the first true "Formula One" championship was run in 1950.

In the 1950s, Formula One cars were like regular passenger cars, with the engine in front. Big changes in car design came in the 1960s and 1970s. By 1961, all Formula One car engines were placed behind the driver. Airfoils, or

An image of the south view of the Grand Prix of Europe in Valencia, Spain.

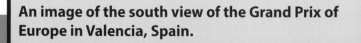

wings, appeared on the cars in the 1970s and gave them more stability.

INDY

Open-wheel racing came to the United States in 1909. The biggest and most popular of these races is the Indianapolis 500 (called the "Indy 500" for short), held in Indiana. The first Indy 500 was held in 1911. The style of cars on the circuit became known as Indy cars, after the famous race.

Indy cars were similar to passenger cars in the early 1900s. Cars had two seats, one for the driver and one for a mechanic. The design of the cars began to change in the 1960s to look more like today's Formula One cars.

Safety features also improved after three drivers and a crew member died as a result of crashes at the Indy 500 in 1972 and 1973. Since then, safety features have constantly been updated to help keep drivers, crew members, and spectators from harm.

In past decades, there were several racing series that included Indy cars. But today, there is just one Indy-type series of races in the United States, the IZOD IndyCar Series. The IZOD IndyCar Series also has three developmental leagues: Firestone Indy Lights, Star Mazda Championship, and U.S. F2000 Championship.

Helio Castroneves of team Penkse cruises around the course at the Detroit Grand Prix in his Shell V-Power/Pennzoil Ultra car.

Like Formula One, IZOD IndyCar Series drivers race for teams owned by companies or sponsors.

CHAMP SERIES

From 1979 to 2004, the Championship Auto Racing Teams (CART) series was a popular series of Indy-type races. But eventually, many of the teams left it to go to the Indy Racing League (IRL), now known as IndyCar.

When the CART series went bankrupt in 2004, some remaining team owners decided to buy it. They renamed it the Champ Car World Series. The Champ Series season ran from March to November. It held 18 events in 2006.

However, in 2008, Champ Car World Series filed for bankruptcy, and agreed to a deal that would combine the Champ Car World Series and the Indy Racing League so that now both are part of the IZOD IndyCar Series.

INDY RACING LEAGUE

The IRL was formed in 1996. Its first season had only four races with many unknown drivers. IRL featured some of the best-known drivers from the United States and other countries.

The IndyCar season now has fifteen races and runs from March to September. The most famous race on the

The final race of the 2006 Champ Car World Series was held in Mexico City. Sebastien Bourdais of France (above) won the race to become that year's champion.

THE MOST FAMOUS RACE IN THE WORLD

The Indianapolis Motor Speedway opened in August 1909. The first race drew a crowd of 80,000. The speedway was later enlarged. It is now the biggest sports arena in the world—it can hold more than 400,000 fans and has permanent seating for more than 250,000! The Indianapolis 500 is the speedway's most famous race.

Up to 33 cars are allowed in the race. Drivers race 200 laps around the 2.5-mile track for a total of 500 miles, which is how the race got its name. Today, drivers speed around at an average of 220 mph.

At one time, the track was paved with bricks. In 1936, asphalt replaced the bricks, but the nickname "The Brickyard" survives.

After the Indy 500, the winner drinks milk. The tradition started in 1936 when winner Louis Meyer drank some milk. A dairy executive saw a photo of this and decided that milk should be a part of every Indy 500 victory celebration.

circuit is the Indy 500. The IRL circuit is also known as IndyCar.

A CHANGING SPORT

The sport of open-wheel racing has gone through many changes, and is still changing all the time. For example, in 2005, Danica Patrick, a twenty-three-year-old woman driver, finished fourth in the Indy 500. It was the best performance by a woman in Indy history, and it drew many new fans to the sport of open-wheel racing. In 2008, Patrick won the Japan 300, becoming the first woman to win a race in the IndyCar series. Soon after, she left IndyCar to race full time in NASCAR.

THE CARS

Formula One and IndyCars are nothing like your family's set of wheels. They are specially built to handle the curves and straight sections, or straightaways, of a racetrack at high speeds.

CHASSIS

An open-wheel car's chassis (CHASS-ee) is made from a strong material called carbon fiber. It forms the main structure—or "skeleton"—of the car. The wheels and engine are attached to the chassis. The chassis must be tough enough to protect the driver in a crash, but light enough to keep from weighing down the car.

TIRES

A regular car tire can last 10,000 miles or more. But a typical open-wheel race car tire will last for only about 120

Tony Kanaan is leading the chase at the Toyota Grand Prix of Long Beach in California in 2011.

miles—at the most. This is because of the extreme pressure, heat, and wear-and-tear of racing at high speeds. Open-wheel race car tires are about twice the size of tires on regular cars and are made of soft rubber to grip the track. Formula One cars used non-treaded "slick" tires until a 1998 rule change. They now ride on grooved tires, to keep speeds down on the corners. This makes racing safer.

IndyCar Series cars still use "slicks." When the car is racing along the track, the tire surface gets so hot that it becomes sticky. This helps the tire grip the ground. However, grooved tires are used in wet weather for safety. They will not slip as much as slicks on a wet track.

ENGINE

Formula One cars use small, powerful engines that produce 830 horsepower (hp). That is about three times as powerful as a regular passenger car. IndyCars use slightly less powerful engines, with roughly 600 hp.

The intense heat and energy put out by any race-car engine almost tears it apart. Rubber parts melt, plastic parts break, and metal parts are heated up enough to weaken them. In the past, each engine used to be rebuilt almost from scratch with new parts after every race because of

IndyCar racers use slicks, which are tires with no grooves (left). Formula One cars use grooved tires (right).

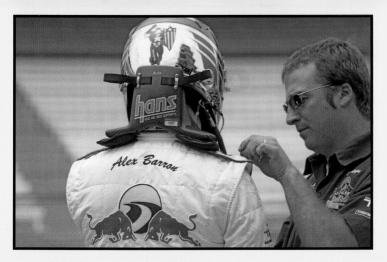

A SAFE COCOON

Inside an open-wheel racer is the cockpit—the driver's "survival cell." Many drivers have walked away from crashes because of the safety features of the survival cell. For example, padded upside-down U-shaped roll bars in front of, and behind the driver shield the driver if the car overturns. The weight of the car will fall on the roll bars and not the driver.

Padding in the cockpit and a helmet protect the driver's head in case of a crash. But the driver must also wear the Head and Neck Support (HANS) device. It is a collar that attaches to the driver's helmet. The HANS device keeps the driver's head and neck from moving around during a race. This reduces the risk of injury.

19

this. But in 2006, all cars in the IRL began using a new engine designed to better withstand the harsh conditions of racing. After each race, these engines are taken apart and the parts are carefully examined to make sure they are still in top shape. Then the engines are rebuilt for the next race, using whatever new parts are necessary.

BODY

While the chassis of an open-wheel racer is like the car's skeleton, the outer shell, or body, is like the car's skin. It is made of lightweight carbon fiber or other high-tech plastic, and fiberglass. The body is also designed to cut cleanly through the air at top speeds. It can be put on and taken off the chassis easily in case it is damaged in a race.

The car's body must be a certain length and height according to the rules of each circuit. This ensures that all of the cars are equal in design and one does not have an advantage over another.

The inside area of the body that holds the driver's cockpit is called the "tub." The body's outside is painted a bright color and covered with the names of the team sponsors.

All Formula One cars have up to five cameras attached to them during every race. The cameras are used during

In 2012, Ferrari released their new F2012 Ferrari Formula One race car with this hi-tech steering wheel.

live television coverage of the races to give fans a racer's-eye view of the action.

WINGS

Airplanes have wings to help get them off the ground. Open-wheel cars have "wings," too, but these wings are attached to the front and rear of the car.

Also, the cars' wings do the opposite of airplane wings. Instead of helping to lift the car off the ground, they press

SMOKIN' FACTS!

Formula One

IndyCar

FORMULA ONE OR INDY: A CLOSER LOOK

	FORMULA 1	INDYCAR
Top Speed	Fastest time ever was 231.5 mph	Fastest official speed was 237.498 mph
Horsepower	700 to 720 hp	650 hp
Tires	Grooved	Ungrooved
Wheelbase	118 1/8 inches to 129 59/64 inches	118 1/8 inches to 122 1/16 inches
Weight	Minimum weight with driver is 1322.774 lbs (600 kg)	Maximum weight without driver and fuel is 1524.982 lbs (691.72 kg)
Height	37 13/32 inches (shown as 950 mm)	38 inches (shown as 965 mm)
Width	Maximum width is 70 7/8 inches with tires inflated (shown as 1800 mm)	Minimum is 77 9/16 inches and maximum is 78 23/64 inches (shown as 1.97m and 1.99m)

CAMERA
ROLL BAR
REAR WING
FRONT WING

Open-wheel race cars have wings, also called airfoils, at the front and rear.

the car harder onto the track. This is called downforce. It gives the car more traction, or ability to stick to the track. This helps the car to speed up, brake, and turn corners.

AT THE TRACK

The goal of any race car driver is to win—plain and simple. Every member of the team works extremely hard at every race to reach that goal.

A lot of hard work goes into getting a team's equipment ready for a race weekend. Races are held all over the world, so teams are always on the go. Formula One and IndyCar teams carry extra cars, spare parts, tires, tools, and computers in huge 18-wheel trucks. Teams arrive at the track on Wednesday or Thursday to set up portable garages for the weekend ahead.

All events start with practice sessions. These sessions are important for all race-car drivers and teams. They give the drivers a feel for the track before the race. It is also the last time the mechanics can work on the cars' brakes, engine, and anything else that may need adjusting.

Drivers and team managers attend a pre-race meeting at every event. Here, the race director goes over the rules and regulations.

A day or two before each race, the drivers must qualify for starting positions. To qualify, the drivers race around the track. The ones with the fastest times get to participate in the race. Their times also determine where the cars line up on the starting grid. (The starting grid is the position the cars take at the start of the race.)

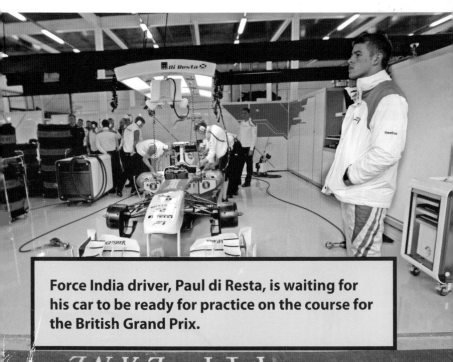

Force India driver, Paul di Resta, is waiting for his car to be ready for practice on the course for the British Grand Prix.

On race day, the drivers line up in the order of how they finished in the qualifying runs.

The driver with the best time gets the best spot—the pole position. This is the inside lane of the first row. The driver in the pole position starts the race in the lead and has the shortest and fastest route around the track for the first lap of the race. The other cars line up two-by-two in rows behind, positioned eight meters (about 26 feet) apart.

TYPES OF TRACKS

Formula One races are about 180 miles long and cannot last longer than two hours. An exception is made if the race is suspended and then restarted. The races are held on different types of courses around the world. Most are on racetracks with straightaways and curves to test the drivers' skills. Some, such as the Monaco Grand Prix in Europe, take place on narrow, curvy city streets that have been closed to traffic. IndyCar races cover distances of 150 to 500 miles and last from two to four hours.

There are three types of tracks—ovals, super ovals, and road courses. Ovals, or speedways, measure between 0.75 and 2.5 miles. The Indy 500 is run on this type of track. Super ovals, or superspeedways, are at least 1.5 miles and have steeply banked (slanted) turns.

The Grand Prix of Monaco is run on a road course that is just over two miles long. It is one of the most difficult courses in Formula One.

WATCH THOSE FLAGS

Colorful flags quickly tell drivers what is going on during a race. Drivers have to look out for the flags, like regular drivers must be on the lookout for traffic signals and road signs.

 START racing!

Take CAUTION—there may be an accident on the track. All drivers must slow down to a lower speed and cannot pass other cars until the track is cleared.

STOP! It could be bad weather or a bad accident, and the race has been stopped. All drivers must leave the track.

 Busted! A driver has gotten a PENALTY for unsafe driving and must leave the track, either for one lap or the rest of the race.

Slower cars must MOVE OVER for faster cars (in Formula One, the flag is plain blue).

 LAST LAP (IndyCar); there is an emergency or a slow-moving vehicle on the track (Formula One).

END OF THE RACE; the first driver to pass this flag is the winner!

The Iowa Corn Indy 250 in Iowa is an example of a race held on an oval, or speedway. Iowa Speedway is home to both IndyCar and NASCAR events.

Road courses are between 1.5 and 4 miles. They can be on a permanent track or on a special track set up on city streets. The Streets of Long Beach race in California is run on city streets that are usually very busy—when they are not cleared for the race!

RACE AND STRATEGY

Speeding along at well over 200 mph, the driver is strapped tightly into the cockpit. The engine roars. The car is vibrating. The inside of the cockpit is like an oven because of the engine's heat. (Cockpit temperatures can reach 120 degrees on hot days!) It is tough to concentrate under these conditions. But a race car driver must stay focused. Formula One races last for two hours. Most IndyCar races last for two hours. The Indy 500 can last even longer—sometimes over three hours.

Drivers must remain aware of their competitors and what they are doing. They have to look out for flags to see what is happening in the race. At the same time, they use their cockpit radios to talk with their crews to tell them how the car is running. Likewise, the crews tell them when to push harder or take it easy.

Drivers have to handle the challenges of different tracks. Racing on longer tracks with a lot of straightaways means more passing. On curved tracks, there is more cornering and braking. Road courses have such tight turns that drivers cannot afford to make any mistakes.

Oil spills, debris on the track, and accidents can happen during a race. When one of these things occurs, the yellow flag is waved. Drivers know to slow down until the track is clear.

To win this race, the drivers are going to have to battle all the way to the finish line.

The race is over when the first car crosses the finish line after all the laps have been run. As the checkered flag drops, the winning team high-fives each other and starts celebrating. The fans shout for their favorites. After a victory lap around the track, the top-finishing cars roll into Victory Lane. Reporters and photographers crowd around to capture the moment. After the drivers climb from their cars and wave to the fans, the winning driver and sometimes the top two finishers receive their trophies in Victory Lane. After an Indy 500 win, it is a tradition for drivers to drink milk. Formula One drivers often spray champagne on their teammates and the reporters.

It has been a hard few hours of driving, and the driver is tired and hot. But he does not feel tired at all if he is standing on that podium holding up a gleaming trophy. . . and getting a big cash prize!

WORKING TOGETHER TO WIN

Besides getting into a good position, a driver must make sure that the car has enough fuel and that the tires have enough grip for the entire race. When it is time to refuel or change tires that have worn out due to the hard racing, the pit crew calls the driver into the pit area. Each team has its own pit area. Drivers can make several pit stops during a race.

A successful pit stop can often be the difference in winning or losing a race. Every team's pit crew is ready for action. Each member has a job to do. A pit crew practices its jobs just as any athlete works on his or her game. A good pit crew can change all four tires and refuel a car in less than ten seconds! The pit crew can be just as important as the driver in winning a race. Together, they work hard to make their team number one.

After team Aston-Martin won, they lined up at the podium. After receiving their prize, they sprayed all of those champagne bottles.

IN THE PITS

As many as twenty-nine or more (but there is no limit) people usually work on a car during a pit stop. These are the basic jobs:

Lollipop man: Coordinates all of the mechanics' work during the pit stop and gets the driver to stop at the exact pit station and informs driver of when his car is ready.

Jack man: Connects an air hose at the rear of the car's chassis to lift it for a tire change.

Rear tire changer (far side): After the tire is changed, this crew member helps push the car out of the pit area.

Rear tire changer (near side): Helps push the car out of the pit area after the tire is changed.

Front tire changer (far side): Guides the driver into the team's pit area. After changing the tire, this crew member adjusts the wings and lets the driver know when to leave the pit.

Front tire changer (far side): Guides the driver into the team's pit area. After changing the tire, this crew member adjusts the wings and lets the driver know when to leave the pit.

Fuel man: Refuels the car by putting the nozzle into the opening of the fuel tank.

Firemen: Crew members who are ready with fire extinguishers in the event that the car catches on fire.

REAL ATHLETES

Car racing requires a lot of endurance. This means that drivers need a lot of strength for a long period of time. Some people argue that race car drivers are not real athletes. But drivers must have strength, stamina, quick reflexes, good vision, and great concentration to perform at their best. Drivers train as hard as other athletes. They run, swim, and bike to stay in shape. They do exercises to build strong arms, necks, and chests. Drivers also watch what they eat. They eat energy-boosting foods and drink lots of water before a race to make sure they have enough stamina. They must stay calm, alert, and levelheaded. They must rely on their quick thinking to make it to the finish line.

Drafting

Race car drivers just drive around in circles, right? Wrong. It takes loads of skill to handle a race car. These are just two of the techniques drivers use on the track:

Drafting: When a car is traveling at 200 mph, it creates a wind tunnel. This reduces the wind resistance for the car directly behind it. That car actually gets sucked along by the wind. A good driver can use this "draft" to pass the car in front or let up on the gas a bit to save fuel.

Cornering: While driving on the straightaways of a racetrack is all about power, turning corners takes a lot of skill. The driver must brake, turn, and then accelerate (speed up) out of the turn. Cornering can be dangerous, and takes practice.

Cornering

THE BEST DRIVERS

Most race car drivers start racing go-karts when they are kids. If they are really good, they can eventually compete at the national level. Then they may move on to international competition. From go-karts, drivers can then progress to other types of racing, such as Formula Three (in Europe), Sprint Car Series, Midget Car Series, and Formula 2000 (in the United States). Then, drivers hope to move up to the "major leagues" of racing: IZOD IndyCar Series or Formula One. They work their way up to the highest level by impressing team owners. They hope the team owners will hire them to race for their team.

Many people consider open-wheel drivers to be the most talented drivers in the world. They have incredible skill and are daring on the track. Here are some of the best racers today:

Scott Dixon edges Helio Castroneves at the Bombardier Learjet 550.

Fernando Alonso, Spain: In 2005, Alonso did something that seemed impossible. He took the Formula One Championship away from Michael Schumacher. It was the first time in five years a driver other than Schumacher had won the crown. At age twenty-four, Alonso became the youngest champion in Formula One history. Alonso went on to win the championship again in 2006. He also finished second in 2010 and 2012.

Dario Franchitti, Scotland: Franchitti is arguably the best IndyCar driver of the century. He has an amazing list of career achievements, including four IZOD IndyCar Series titles, (2007, 2009–11), and three Indianapolis 500 victories. Franchitti dedicated his 2012 Indy 500 win to his best friend Dan Wheldon, who had died in a fifteen-car wreck in the last race of 2011. Franchitti had 31 career victories through the 2012 season, good for 7th place all-time.

Sebastian Vettel, Germany: Vettel has truly made a name for himself by winning the Formula One Championship each year from 2010 to 2012. He became the youngest to win the Formula One Championship, and is also the youngest to win two championships! Not bad for a guy who only started racing in Formula One in 2008.

Sebastian Vettel is among today's best Formula One drivers.

Tony Kanaan, Brazil: Kanaan won the 2004 IRL Championship. He had 15-straight top-five finishes, including three wins and six second-place finishes. Kanaan completed all 3,305 laps of the races he was in—the first IndyCar driver to do so. Through the start of the 2013 season, he's won 15 races, including the 2013 Indy 500.

A DRIVER'S GEAR

Drivers are covered from head to toe with gear for protection in case of fire.

Helmet: A padded helmet covers the driver's face completely. It is made of carbon fiber material, similar to a race car's chassis and body.

Driving suit: A driver must wear a one-piece fire-resistant suit. Even the underwear is fire-resistant!

Balaclava: This fire-resistant hood is worn under the helmet. It is more protection for the driver's head.

Shoes: Shoes are made of leather or suede. They are lined with fire-resistant material and have rubber soles for grip.

Gloves: Fire-resistant gloves have leather palms for gripping the steering wheel.

WHAT ABOUT WOMEN RACERS?

Many women have played a part as drivers in open-wheel racing. A few have made their mark at the Indy 500.

Janet Guthrie: In 1977, Guthrie was the first woman to start in the Indy 500. She raced two more times (1978 and 1979). Guthrie's best finish was ninth place in 1978. When she qualified for Indy in 1978, Guthrie broke her own women's world record. She raised the record to 191.002 mph.

Lyn St. James: St. James competed in the Indy 500 seven times (1992–1997, 2000), the most of any woman. St. James finished 11th in 1992 and was named the Indy 500 Rookie of the Year; the first woman to receive that honor. She set the women's world record in closed-course speed in 1995; reaching 225.722 mph. St. James earned more than $1 million competing in the Indy 500.

Sarah Fisher: Fisher started her first Indy 500 race in 2000 at age nineteen. She was the youngest woman and third-youngest driver ever to compete in the race. Fisher participated in the race for the next four years. Her best finish was 21st place in 2004. Fisher's Indy 500 earnings total more than $1 million.

Danica Patrick: The IRL got a boost in popularity with Patrick's success. She was named IRL Rookie of the Year in 2005 after finishing fourth in the Indy 500. It was the best finish for a woman in the history of the race. Patrick led the race for 19 laps, becoming the only woman to lead the Indy field. She finished eighth in 2006. She became the only woman ever to win a race in the IndyCar Series when she won the Japan 300 in 2008. In 2009, she recorded the highest finish for a woman in Indianapolis 500 history by finishing in 3rd place. Danica currently races in the NASCAR Sprint Cup Series.

Currently, there are four women racing in the IZOD IndyCar Series: Simona de Silvestro, Katherine Legge, Pippa Mann, and Ana Beatriz. Through the middle of the 2013 season, Silvestro had the most success, earning eight career Top 10 finishes and one Top 5. Legge became a rookie in the IZOD IndyCar Series in 2012 and is the first woman to win the British Racing Driver's Club Rising Star award. Beatriz is continuing to get better each week.

ALL-TIME BEST

Michael Schumacher, Germany: Schumacher was the best in Formula One racing from the mid-1990s to his first retirement in 2006. He won the driver's championship a record seven times (1994, 1995, and 2000–04). Schumacher came out of retirement in 2010 and raced for team Mercedes for three seasons.

Mario Andretti, United States: Andretti is often called the greatest race car driver in history. He is certainly the best all-around driver. Andretti is the only driver to win the Daytona 500, a NASCAR race (1967), the Indy 500 (1969), and the Formula One Championship (1978). He is also a four-time IndyCar champion (1965, 1966, 1969, and 1984). In 1993, Andretti became the oldest winner in IndyCar history at fifty-three years and thirty-four days. He retired in 1994.

A.J. Foyt, United States: Foyt is the only driver to win the Indy 500, the 24 Hours of Le Mans, and the Daytona 500. He is the first driver to win the Indy 500 four times (1961, 1964, 1967, and 1977). Foyt won the season championship seven times and is the all-time leader in victories with 67. Foyt retired in 1993.

Rick Mears, United States: Mears won the Indy 500 four times (1979, 1984, 1988, and 1991). Mears also won three CART championships (1979, 1981, and 1982). He retired from racing in 1992.

Today, a future group of world-class drivers is busy perfecting its skills in the "minor leagues" of open-wheel racing. Those drivers will work until they are good enough to compete against the best in the world.

Rick Mears celebrates on his car after breaking a track speed record during a qualifying run.

AIRFOILS—Wings that are attached to the front and rear of a race car for stability.

ASPHALT—Tar-like substance mixed with sand and gravel that is used to pave racetracks.

BALACLAVA—A fire-resistant hood that drivers wear under their helmets.

CARBON FIBER—A strong but lightweight material used to make the chassis and body of a race car.

CHASSIS—The skeleton or frame of a car.

COCKPIT—The area of the chassis where the driver sits.

DOWNFORCE—The pressure created when air pushes a car's tires to the ground.

GRID—The starting order of cars in a race, determined by qualifying times.

GRIP—A car's ability to stay in contact with the racetrack when accelerating, braking, and turning a corner.

HANS DEVICE—Short for Head and Neck Support device, it's a safety collar worn by drivers to keep the head and neck stable during a race. This reduces the risk of head and neck injuries.

HORSEPOWER (HP)—A measure of engine performance and power. It compares the power created by one horse to what an engine can do. For example, it would take 720 horses working together to create the same power as a 720-hp Formula One engine.

PIT CREW—Members of a driver's team who maintain, refuel, and change the tires on the car during a race.

POLE POSITION—The spot where the driver with the fastest qualifying time starts the race. It is the inside of the front row, which is the shortest distance around the track.

SLICKS—Ungrooved racing tires used by Champ Series, Indy Racing League, and IZOD IndyCar Series cars.

STRAIGHTAWAYS—The straight sections of a racetrack.

VICTORY LANE—Part of the track reserved for the race winner and the top finishers to park their cars and stand on a platform to receive their trophies.

BOOKS

Davidson, Donald, and Rick Shaffer. *Autocourse Official Illustrated History of the Indianapolis 500: Revised and Updated Second Edition.* Worcestshire, UK: Icon Publishing, Ltd., 2013.

Georgiou, Tyrone. *Indy Cars.* New York: Gareth Stevens Pub., 2012.

Palmer, Tom. *Formula 1: Go Turbo.* London: Franklin Watts, 2012.

Smith, Roger. *Formula 1: All the Races-2nd Edition: The World Championship Story Race-By-Race: 1950–2012.* Sparkford, England: Haynes Publishing, 2013.

INTERNET ADDRESSES

HISTORY OF FORMULA 1

http://www.grandprixhistory.org/story1.htm
The history of Formula 1 racing, and how it was once called Grand Prix.

THE OFFICIAL F1 WEB SITE

http://www.formula1.com/default.html

THE OFFICIAL SITE OF INDYCAR

http://www.indycar.com
IndyCar fans can participate in lots of online activities on this official Web site.